Exhibit

And as each new age
is convinced that it
constitutes what is normal,
that it represents the true
condition of things, the
people of the new age soon
began to imagine the people
of the previous one as an
exact replica of themselves,
in exactly the same setting.

— Karl Ove Knausgård,
A Time for Everything

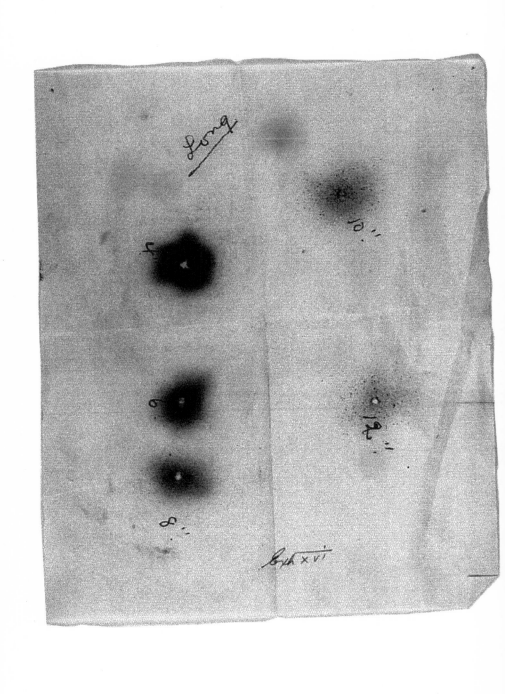

Table of Contents

4 inches

4 inches

6 inches

6 inches

8 inches

8 inches

1360

EXHIBIT

"A"

EVIDENCE TAKEN AT INQUEST HELD ON THE BODY OF ALEX MCPHAIL ON DECEMBER 21ST, AT THE ALBERTA PROVINCIAL POLICE BARRACKS, DRUMHELLER / THERE ARE TWO SHACKS THERE / IN THE EAST SHACK, THE DIMENSIONS OF WHICH ARE 12 X 16 FT. I FOUND THE BODY OF ALEX MCPHAIL / THE BODY WAS THIRTY THREE OR THIRTY FOUR INCHES FROM THE DOOR WITH THE HEAD TOWARDS THE NORTH / THE HEAD WAS IN THE DIRECTION OF THE FENCE WE CAME THROUGH GOING TO THE HOUSE / THE DOOR OPENS INWARDS / THE HEAD WAS LYING TOWARDS THE HANDLE OF THE DOOR / THE FIRST THING ABOUT THE BODY YOU WOULD SEE WOULD BE THE HAND AND THE UPPER PART OF THE BODY / THE BODY WAS DRESSED AS FOLLOWS: A BROWN KHAKI SHIRT AND AN UNDERVEST / THE LOWER PART WAS CLOTHED WITH UNDERPANTS, TROUSERS AND OVERALLS / THROWN ACROSS THE LOWER PART OF THE BODY WAS SEVERAL COATS AND A SHEET / THERE WERE NO SHOES OR STOCKINGS ON THE DECEASED / UNDER THE HEAD WAS A PILLOW BLOOD SATURATED / THE SHIRT AND UNDERSHIRT WERE BOTH OPEN AT THE NECK, AND UP FROM THE BOTTOM ABOUT SIX OR EIGHT INCHES / THE OVERALLS, PANTS AND UNDERCLOTHES WERE DOWN TO THE KNEES LEAVING THE UPPER PART OF THE LEGS, HIPS AND ABDOMEN EXPOSED / I DID NOT SEE ANY SIGN OF BLOOD INSIDE OR OUTSIDE OF THE PAIR OF DRAWERS MARKED **EXHIBIT** I / I DO NOT SEE ANY SIGN OF BLOOD INSIDE OR OUTSIDE OF THE TROUSERS MARKED **EXHIBIT** II / I DID NOT SEE ANY SIGN OF BLOOD ON THE INSIDE OR OUTSIDE OF THE OVERALLS MARKED **EXHIBIT** III / I AM OF THE OPINION THAT THE HOLE IN THE BIB OF HE OVERALLS IS A BULLET HOLE / IN **EXHIBIT** I UNDERDRAWERS THE BLOOD STAIN IS IN MY OPINION A BLOOD STAIN BY SOMEONE TOUCHING IT WITH A BLOODY FINGER / **EXHIBIT** IV UNDERSHIRT I DO NOT SEE ANY BULLET IN THIS / THE UNDERSHIRT COULD NOT BE PULLED DOWN SO THAT THE OPENING IN FRONT WOULD BE BELOW THE BULLET HOLE IN THE CHEST, **EXHIBIT** V / THAT GARMENT WAS THE OUTER SHIRT ON THE DECEASED / IT WAS CUT UP THE BACK BY ME / THERE IS A HOLE OPPOSITE THE LOWER BUTTON OF THE SHIRT / I WOULD JUDGE THE SHIRT WAS BUTTONED WHEN THE BULLET WAS FIRED / I DO NOT FIND ANY BLOOD LOWER THAN THE PERFORATION / THE TEAR AT THE BOTTOM OF THE OPENING IN FRONT WAS THERE WHEN I SAW HIM FIRST. / IN THE MID-LINE OF THE CHEST THERE WAS A BULLET WOUND, ALSO A BULLET HOLE IN THE RIGHT TEMPLE / ON THE FLOOR ABOUT THE HEAD WAS A POOL OF BLOOD / THERE WAS NO BLOOD ABOUT THE FEET OR THE MIDDLE OF THE

BODY. THERE WAS BLOOD ON THE UTENSILS (KITCHEN) ABOUT THE ROOM / THERE WAS NO OTHER BLOOD EXCEPT ON RAGS LYING AROUND. I VISITED THE SHACK AGAIN ON FRIDAY LAST / I SAW A BLOOD STAINED NEWSPAPER IN THE DIRECTION I CALLED NORTH / THERE WAS A CONSIDERABLE AMOUNT OF BLOOD / THIS WOULD BE ABOUT FOUR FEET FROM WHERE WE FOUND THE BODY / IN THE SHACK WAS A BED IN THE S.E. CORNER OF THE SHACK / **EXHIBIT** VI IS A DIAGRAM WHICH I DREW WHILE OUT THERE / THE CONTENTS FAIRLY WELL FILLED THE SHACK / ABOUT EIGHTEEN INCHES FROM THE FEET OF THE BODY AND AT A FOOT OF A DRESSER AND CLOSE TO A BOX OF EGGS, I FOUND A .22 CALIBER CARTRIDGE SHELL, EMPTY / I FOUND QUITE A NUMBER OF LOADED SHELLS ON THE DRESSER / **EXHIBIT** VII IS THE EMPTY SHELL I FOUND / I FOUND A RIFLE BEHIND THE SHACK / THIS PLACE IS MARKED ON **EXHIBIT** VI / IN THE OTHER SHACK WEST OF THE ONE WHERE I FOUND THE BODY WAS MISS MCPHAIL'S SHACK / THE SHACKS ARE ABOUT TEN FEET APART / SHEET NO. 2 / I DID NOT MEASURE THE DISTANCE / THE DOOR GOING INTO HER SHACK WAS DIRECTLY OPPOSITE THE DOOR INTO THE OTHER / I SAW A RED SWEATER ACROSS THE FEET OF THE DECEASED ON THURSDAY / I FOUND NO SOCKS IN THE SHACK ON THURSDAY / I FOUND A PAIR OF BOOTS A FOOT FROM HIS FEET / **EXHIBIT** VIII IS THE RIFLE FOUND OUTSIDE THE SHACK BY CONSTABLE IRVING / IT IS A TWENTY CALIBER SINGLE SHOT RIFLE / THE EJECTOR WILL NOT WORK, OTHERWISE IT IS IN GOOD ORDER / IF A MAN WERE FIRING TWO SHOTS HE WOULD HAVE TO PULL BACK THE LEVER AND THE SHELL WOULD EJECT / IF IT DID NOT HE WOULD HAVE TO GET IT OUT SOME OTHER WAY / HE WOULD THEN RELOAD / I WOULD SAY IT COULD BE DONE IN A MINUTE IF HE HAD NO DELAY / IT MAY TAKE HIM LONGER / I FOUND THIS EXPLODED SHELL IN THE GUN WHEN IT WAS FOUND. I HAD AN INTERVIEW WITH HIS SISTER BEFORE I WENT TO THE FARM / THERE WAS THE HANDLE OF A TABLE SPOON IN THE MAN'S MOUTH WHEN HIS BODY WAS FOUND / IN MISS MCPHAIL'S SHACK WERE FOUND THREE LONG AND THREE SHORT TWENTY TWO RIFLE SHELLS LOADED / ON A CHAIR WAS FOUND A MAN'S UNDERCLOTHES / THE BED CLOTHES ON THE BED WERE IN AN UNTIDY CONDITION / I WOULD THINK SOMEONE HAD BEEN SITTING OR LYING ON IT / THERE WERE TWO WINDOWS IN THIS SHACK / I DID NOT SEE ANY KNIFE IN THE ROOM WHICH COULD HAVE BEEN USED TO PRY OUT THE SHELL / EVERY TIME THE CHEST OR STOMACH WAS TOUCHED BLOOD WOULD OOZE FROM THE MOUTH OF THE DECEASED / SIGNED J. BURTON

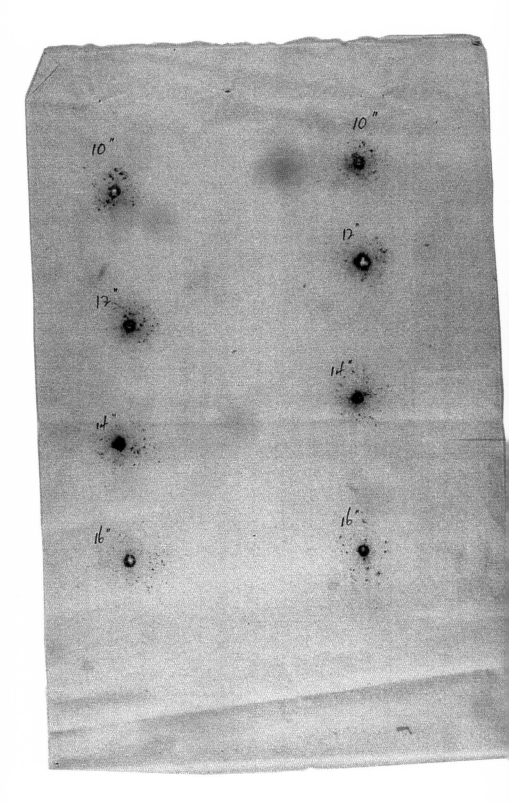

EXHIBIT

"B"

Dwelling

the house is like a box where the walls fit snugly round the figures and there can be a really tight fit. the children move out of their cosmically rounded dwelling into their early house of the cube.

windows appear now as well as doors. the view extends towards the outside. the chimney-pot smokes, it is nice and warm and the figure on the bed relaxes.

the walls are opened up; one is now not only in the house but at the same time one also faces the house. the outside of the house appears.

Q. *What did you first notice?*

I saw dark tucked inside a sleeve, more under a pot, more dark walking along the ledge below the window, more pawing at the walls, pushing into corners, crouching at the rear of a cage, fitting into a box, a stack of black jaws coming in wet. More dark coming in with a dry and wet coat, more went behind the door, more was there, was behind the door, the background was becoming

the cat. The cat becoming the background. The shack was as square as a perfect block. It suggested nothing. Triangles in the dusty red hair combings and polygons in the spilled face powder, like curtains wavering around in elliptical curves. Dark flattening the stacks of black crates, black boxes, black blocks. Dark in the stacks of rings in the tree stump serving as a kitchen table. Even in the lens flares like in the giant close-up of Norman Bates' eye, the inhuman eyes of the cyborg, the terrified eyes of the citizens under surveillance.

The fact of being orange occurs at the nose of the cat
The property "that it is orange" is in the locus of the cat's nose
Orangeness is in the cat's nose
The cat's nose has an orange colour
The cat's nose is orange.

I went when I saw the cat
I saw the cat when I went
When I saw the cat I went
When I went I saw the cat.

It was as dark as black silage and as dark as the tyre on the roof. It was as dark as a stack of black cats in the shack. As dark as the stack of crows on the doorstep

Ice blond

Margaret is devoid of colour, ice blond
with hair in a bun spun like a vortex
She prods stars along the sky with a stick
looks for smoke plumes that come
from birds that ignite in midair
She is footage projected upside down
With her feet, she retrieves the streamers, their feathers
charred too severely for flight
and then stays out in the rain picking carrots
and then stays out in the rain picking carrots

Ready camera

Camera one dolly in—hold it. Ready camera two for pan shot of speaker as she walks. Cut to two. Camera one dolly back ready for long shot of speaker when she turns. Cut to one. Ready camera three for medium profile of speaker:

> "i combed my hair and put some coal on the stove. i was lying down on the bed partly dressed for awhile, and just looking out of the window when i thought i heard a sob. i went over to see what it was. i looked out of the window from the bed."

Margaret parts the curtains onto a 180° pan shot of waves on the beach fading into a
pan shot of a cheering crowd fading into a
pan shot of a wheat field fading into a
pan shot of Geng Biao, Xu Deheng, Zhu Xuefan, Banqen Erdini Qoigyi Gyancan, Zhou Gucheng, Hu Yuzhi, and Han Xianchu sitting in the front row of a rostrum fading into a
pan shot of red scarves being pulled out of tuxedo pockets fading into a
slow pan shot of a carnival in the distance from under a bridge fading into a
pan shot of the bridge fading into a
L to R pan shot of a Welsh valley, its pit buildings and village. This shot pulls back and down, coming closer to the rooftops with their clusters of aerials fading into a

pan shot of an audience revealing spectators evidently delighted with the show and unaware anything is amiss with the star. She appears to regain something of her form.

The rain says

the first raindrops go *ploomp*. long marks across the paper.
margaret cranks a wooden shaft that rubs lightly against a heavy
piece of canvas. the wind soon stands upright. a soft colour-
drawing of lightning bolts flashes across a dark sky above fields
and a farm. dots everywhere. margaret turns a hopper that drops
bird seed onto a piece of stretched wax paper. on the old tin roof
of the garden shed the raindrops all talk at once and say, *ping ping
pinading, ping ping ping ping ping*. seeds from a dandelion are
knocked loose, flow over the birds and their feathers begin to glow
with colour.
margaret draws a large piece of amber through a woollen cloth.
against an umbrella, the rain says *bup bup*. margaret vibrates
the large piece of thin copper sheeting suspended from a frame
by wires. margaret drops flashlight bulbs into a glass. then she is
tucked into bed, listening to the rain going *drum-a-tum* on the
roof above her. during the night, someone sweeps a stiff wire brush
over the rough holes punched in a piece of tin. in the morning,
there is a wet sparkle caught on some spider webs and flowers,
and margaret looks for a rainbow. The pebbles that fall down the
chimney *spit* and *sizzle* on the logs.

Pleasant enough

i looked at him and he seemed pleasant enough. he seemed as if he had forgotten about what he was talking about in the afternoon

Q. What had you been talking about?

dreams

Dreams

i dreamed that we were due to go on a trip with some friends and, and then i didn't know what to wear, and i was upset because i didn't know what to wear. it was supposed to be a trip in the woods. i had to put on a skirt but could not find it. i found a pair of trousers that were too small for me. the friends were making lunch. we were at home. there were seven cats playing around.

there was a witch that made us turn old, and afterwards she leaned out from the window and i saw grandmother L., but she was not grandmother L., she was an angel that looked like grandmother, then grandmother, the true one, was already there at the market, but she really was the true one and the other one was false, and then there was me, crying and crying.

my mother told me, 'A., go buy the bread.' and so i went to buy bread, but when i got in i saw there was nobody in the bakery, there was nobody not even that lady, then i got in and saw a witch, then i went to mother and said, 'mum, there's a witch inside!' and that's all.

Turned outward

A

alex dreams, as if a hard skin were drawn over the tips of the
fingers. as if the legs are enclosed in an elastic stocking. as if food

formed itself into lumps with hard surfaces and angles. as if an
animal were crying in the abdomen. as of an animal wriggling in

the epigastric region. as if animals were floundering about. as if a
splinter of bone were sticking. when alex says anything it is as if

another person had said it. when he sees anything it is as if
another person had seen it. dreams, as if ants were crawling in the

extremities, deep in the muscles and skin. dreams, as if from ants
crawling on the tongue. as if everything were coming out at the

anus. as if drops of cold water were falling from the anus. as of a
warm fluid escaping from the anus. as of a knife sawing up and

down. he could not sit, stand or lie. the only possible position was
kneeling. the anus felt as if it stood wide open. burning, as if

pepper was sprinkled on it. he felt a triangle in his face—the base
formed by the two malar bones, the apex in the vertex. dreams, as

if an apple core were sticking in it. he quickly extends an arm as if
to smooth a dress, and so on the whole day. dreams, that protrude

here and there as if from the arms of a foetus. as if a hot iron were
thrust through it. he felt as if his arm did not belong to him.

dreams, as if from a galvanic battery. dreams, as if a cold wind
blowing on them. he felt sensation in the arms and feet as if they

were turned out-ward. as of steel arrows from forehead to nape of
neck. as if arrows were forced through his breasts. as if blood in his

arteries were boiling hot. as if a lump or a bubble started from the
heart and was forced through the arteries. the arteries in his head

felt as distinct as if they had been vivisected out and were on
display. he heard noise in the right carotid artery as if from

escaping steam. shocks in his ears as of distant artillery. dreams,
as if a ball were coming up in the throat. as if a round body were

ascending from the stomach. as if the feet were going up with the
head remaining still. as if a half-fluid body were ascending in the

throat. as if the right ear were asleep. dreams, the feeling as if after
eating persimmons. the back of his head began to sink. the eyes

were blurry, as if dosed with atropine. dreams, as if they were
poured into an empty barrel. dreams, as if they were beaten

with an axe.

B

alex feels pleasant enough, except for the searing balls that are
dropping from inside each breast through to the back, rolling

down the back, along each leg and dropping off the heels; this
alternates with sensations as if balls of ice are following the same

course. except that the flesh is slack on the lower part of the back.
except that his eye is being drawn backwards by a string. except

that the intestines are rolled up in a ball in the side of the
abdomen. he draws himself up in bed like a ball. he feels pleasant

enough except that his brain is pressing into a ball. except for the
ball rising from the throat into the brain. except that the urinary

organs are being pressed out, twisting and turning, as if by a great
worm. a thick fog lay before his eyes. pearls around his mouth.

pleasant enough except that his body is glass and would break
easily. he feels as if he is sinking deep down in bed. as if the body

is made up of sweets. he perceives a pulse in his body; as if it were
the tick of a watch. he feels pleasant enough except that he is

sitting on a ball, that his parts are made of wood, that his brain
moves as if by boiling water, balancing to and fro, being beaten

with thousands of little hammers. except that the brain is boiling
over and lifting the cranial arch like the lid of a tea-kettle. except

that large cords are drawn to each centre of the hemisphere and
cerebellum from every part of the lobes and cerebellum; as if

tensive pains would break when suddenly they relax and a
bubbling sensation passes from the centres to the circumferences.

he feels as if the brain will crack open the skull, that his brain is
cut to pieces on stooping. he feels pleasant enough except that his

brain seems to go round and round and the eyes move to and fro
as if they went round with the whirling. except that a cord is

stretched tightly from the back of the eyeballs to the center of the
brain. he feels smoke in the brain. he feels pleasant enough except

that the anterior half of his brain is turning in a circle as if he had
been placed in a coal screen and whirled around two or three

times. he smells as if he is made of wet brass, tastes bread on the
tongue. he feels as if in the hands of a stronger power, and

charmed as if he can not break the spell. a noise is felt at every step
as of the breaking of a finger-nail. except for the glass

breaking in his ear. except that his cornea has been breathed upon
so as to dim its lustre. except that a sponge is hanging in his

throat. except that a bunch of his hair is electrified. he feels that
the touch of a comb or brush when rubbing over the scalp goes

into the very brain. he repeatedly passes his hand over his face as if
trying to brush something off. he feels pleasant enough except

for the bug crawling over his lower lip, at 4 AM. he senses a bug
creeping out of his rectum. he feels pleasant enough except for a

bullet lodged at the pit of his stomach. he feels a lightness or
buoyancy, as if he were raised from the ground and could fly away.

on the parts he scratches are innumerable white elevations on a
reddish base, as if in nettlerash, which when deeply scratched

display in the centre a drop of blood the size of a pin head and
burn as if a bright coal lay upon them. he feels pleasant enough

except for the lump of lead on top of his head. except for the
sediment in his urine, like clay, as if the clay was burnt on the

bottom of a vessel. he felt as if a button were pressed on his head.
he does not recognize his friends and family, calling

bystanders as if absent. he feels pleasant enough except for the
headaches, as if the head would burst with dazzling of the eyes

from the sunlight.

C

as if buttermilk and cabbage. as if the body was held in a wire cage.
as if the blood is caged in wires. as if a cold wind. he wakes

up as if called and sees a ghost, which instantly enlarges and then
vanishes. alex moves his hand as if endeavouring to seize some

object which he perceives in the air. in the chest as if from the
purring of a cat. of a noise or movement like purring of a cat

in the region of the stomach. as if a centipede in the left nostril. as
if everything had stopped and he would instantly fall into a sound

sleep, from which he would awaken completely mesmerized. as if
the anterior half of his brain were turning in a circle. he appears

to himself as if chained to his surroundings. as if the chair on
which he is sitting were rising and as if he were looking down.

tongue as white as chalk; as if painted white. his urine as if stirred
up with chalk. as if a piece of chamois skin covered the posterior

part of the tongue. as if after drinking champagne. beautiful
images present themselves to him as if by a charm. his chin feels

as if it is too long. he makes a chirping, roaring and a hammering
sound, as if choked by hands. as if a hand around his elbow. he

is all the time pushing the finger down his throat. as if caused by
icy cold insects with claws. as if a bird's claws were clasping the

knees. his urine, after standing, is thick as if mixed with clay. as of
something opening and shifting within the eyes. during the night

his anus is firmly closed as if locked up. as if the trachea were
closed with a leaf. his hat is pressed upon his head like a weight,

and he continues to feel the sensation even after taking it off. there
is a darkness before his eyes, as if objects were encircled in a

cloud. as if a heavy black cloud has settled all over him, and
enveloped his head, so that all is darkness and confusion. black

moons hover before his eyes, everything is surrounded by mist, as
if covered by cobweb. as of a cobweb on the skin of his face and

hands. cold air is blowing upon his brain. as of a cold wind
blowing under the eyelids. even in a warm room he must bind the

eye with a cloth to protect it. as if touched by a cold metallic object
on the small space over the root of the nose. trembling like

a boiling and seething as if the parts are going to sleep, or as if
becoming drunk. flickering before the eyes as of various colors,

glittering needles, visions of smoke or fog. he is uncertain in his
gait. in looking down it seems as if all objects are commingled. he

has a great sadness. as if he has committed a crime, ending in
weeping, even before strangers. a screw behind each ear. as if

tossed on a rough sea, black dots fill the visual field. violent
tremblings all over. as if he has inhaled sulphur fumes. he

complains of a constrictive pain in the the forehead, as if a small
spot, the size of a dime, is daily contracting and getting smaller,

he thinks that as soon as it is drawn together he will be crazy. as if
feather dust were in the throat. not enough room in the head. a

tympanic note in the stomach. as if the head were lifting off. as if
the scalp were clutched and drawn together to the centre point of

a circle. the taste in his mouth, as if after eating onions. as if a cord
were stretched tightly from the back of the eyeballs to the centre

of the brain. drawing together of the eyes as if by a cord. food
turns like a corkscrew. he must wink. the lungs are stuffed with

cotton. the mouth is filled with cotton. something is laying before
his ear. as if he has something in his mouth, as if the posterior

organs of speech are covered and clumsy. as if from bending tinsel, in temples, forehead. his skin is cracked in small sections and is

flaky as if flour had been sprinkled in the cracks, with the edges turning up. as if swung to and fro in a swing or cradle. a mouse

crawling under the skin in the arm. running and crawling in the bowels. as if ants are in the brain. his whole brain feels as if tired,

gone to sleep and crawling. as if from the crawling of a fly. as though a fly is crawling upon the arms, especially in the bend of

the elbows. crawling in the eyes. a fly crawling on the face. in all the fingers, as if from worms. as though insects were crawling over

the back and in the hair. as if a bunch of hair were electrified, with crawling and bristling of the hair. a centipede in the left nostril. a

worm crawling up the esophagus. this crazy feeling seems to run up the back of the head and feels as if the whole head would be

torn to pieces with great fulness pressing out. his face changes expression and his eyes too. he must feel in motion day and night.

the brain feels as if it was stirred up. as if the "crazy-bone" had been struck. as if he would creep into himself. creeping sensation

in the back as if a soft air were blowing through it. fear and dread
as if something were creeping out of every corner. creeping as if

in the roots of the hair. as of ants creeping in the limbs. fluttering
between the shoulders. creeping of a snake over the entire region

of the short ribs on the left side. as if something were running or
creeping. as if it were a worm creeping up from the pit of his

stomach. he hears a twittering sound as if from a cricket, heard
while in bed in the morning. the skin of his cheek feels tense, hot

and crisp as if it would crack. rumbling and croaking in the
bowels

as of frogs. croaking as of frogs in the abdomen. as if an animal
were crying in it. as if he would creep into himself. as if a crowbar

was pressed tightly from the right to the left breast until it comes
twisted in a knot around the heart. a crowding sensation in the

veins. as if his heart were bound down, or had not room enough
to beat, or as if bolts were holding it. as if the teeth are crushed into

fragments. noises in the ears as of whistling, or crying of animals.
as if a dull stick presses on the parts and is moving in diverse

curved lines.

D

he felt as if the sheets were damp. as of damp clothes on the spine.
he stood firmly, but the things around him seemed to be moving

as if in a confused dance. when walking he felt as if dancing up
and down, as if he must fly. he sees only halves of objects, the

other halves as if covered with dark bodies. he feels as if fire were
darting out of his eyes when walking in the sun or in the room. he

sees colours, as of the rainbow, or is dazzled on looking at bright
objects. he feels as if someone is poking him with a finger in

various parts of the body. he awakens as if from complete absence
of mind, does not know where he is, nor what to answer. he thinks

he is riding on an ox, uses a stick for a gun. he talks of dogs as if
they swarmed about him. he feels as if his eyes are filled with

smoke. black dots fill the visual field. the black letters seem to him
grey and as if a second one of the same light-grey colour were

placed sideways or above. all things were going round and
swimming before the eyes. his iris was first a beautiful brown

color, afterwards it became dim and as if blotted out.

I

he has a grain of sand at the outer angle of the cornea.

L

the eyetooth feels too long and too loose, and feels as if it were
asleep. there is something loose in the head diagonally across the

top. his eyes are hung loosely on a string. a button in the throat,
feels as if it might loosen but does not. he picks at bedclothes as if

looking for something lost, with confused muttering. when sitting
he breathes as if asleep. trembles internally with an urge as if he

must gradually talk louder and faster. luminous lights or sparks
fall down alongside of the eye. a hen's egg, rising and falling. he can

only pass stool by leaning very far back. ice-water rises and falls
through a cylindrical opening in the left lung. he lies in bed as if

intoxicated. he cannot lie on the left side on account of the
sensation as if something were dragging over to that side.

lymphatic glands circle the neck as if they were a string of beads.

M

roaring in the ears as if from machinery. mad and furious as if
drunk. he rolls about the floor as if mad. sensation as if he would

go mad. drawing in the forehead in tow lines, the glabella drawn
outward as if from a magnet. he feels as if he were suffering from

partially developed malaria. sensations as of a triangle in the face.
while awake he talks irrationally as if a man were present. laughs

as if he was tickled.

All bunk

A.

he asked if i felt anything wrong around here. i said no, i didn't feel anything like that. he was talking about the devil and the end of the world. i told him there was no such thing. i told him it was all bunk.

Marmalade on toast

i didn't hear nothing at all, after the thing happened, many people talking about it—the blue haze, but i didn't hear it, me right down under a mountain, nothing to hear and not studying nothing. so when i look outside, outside just as you see, it just like nothing ever happened, outside cool and calm and everything, but when i got out of the house and i looked all around, the devil came walking up the road, leaving hairy footprints as he came, and the paint just started caking up, blistering and the shingles just, they started melting while i was watching. and the devil cussed the whole world out.

the devil came running and sweat poured off him and sparks fell from his eyes and the sweat and the sparks moved around the bends on the road like vehicles. but the sparks, margaret said, came from light coming off the spokes of a wheel and the sweat from over-stewed tea which spilled from the cups that rattled in saucers. and the devil cussed the whole world out.

the ground was baked hard like clay. i felt the heat through the soles of my shoes walking on the ash and had to move away or retrace my steps. the glass windows melted like plastic. China ornaments were melted. i saw a lamp pole burning on the ground. the fine ash was fluidized when walked upon. it was dark and ominous and rolling and you could see, the pulse-like movement at the base. it melted the door knob and the door stood up pretty well. bare earth could be seen on little high points because of the wind.

the devil ran off toward the house with his head thrown back, looking at the sky. his left foot tripped over something, but he didn't look down. his right foot tripped over something, but he didn't look down. and the devil cussed the whole world out.

the devil began sniffing and bees crawled up his nose, and he got a lot of ash, shirt was full of ash, and couldn't see the colour of his red shirt. he said ash was white, first in fine bits like rain, i no get no burn, but the ash kept me warm, ash fall on me and cover me right down so i could't see my fingernails, was grey and black, one mighty cloud, so then i tell myself, i still have to put my foots on the ground. and the devil cussed the whole world out.

it came down sly and sneaky. marmalade on toast. the sky at sunset. then it travelled faster than a car, no car could escape. the pieces of fire were small. must be the end of the world. gas bottles blew and went *pow pow pow pow*. the bricks of the neighbours house took over the whole place like a mighty sea.

heavy ash flung black like black cloth, but i knew it was only an owl holding a dead crow. fire was pitching on the road by the school, but i knew that they were only dimmed light bulbs the devil thinks himself to be a great magician. and he cussed the whole world out.

the devil threw himself to the ground and turned cartwheels until
rolling clouds hung over the farms. the clouds started to reverse.
the clouds were white, black and red from burning but mostly
blackness. they stood up and seemed to roll back. it was all blue
and brown. with fire spinning like a top, from top to bottom.
it is in this tornado that the devil has a one year-old son who is
sleeping in a gold cradle.

the devil ran until he came to a blacksmith shop. he said to the
blacksmith, "fix this hairy tongue of mine. it gets everything
mixed up. and my voice sounds bad too. like carrots and
tangerines. like the sun and cream of tomato soup. like the inside
of a pumpkin and new rust." and with his bagful of walnuts, the
devil somersaulted in anger and cussed the whole world out.

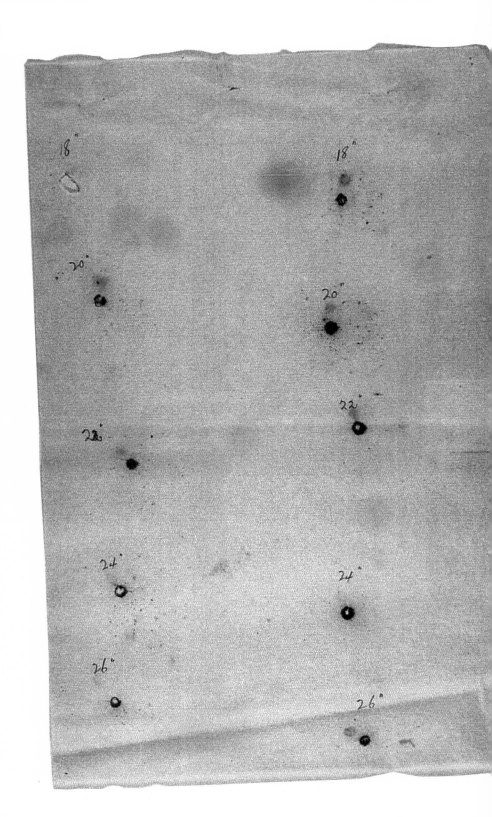

EXHIBIT

"C"

Q. You thought it was a shot, didn't you?
A. No, i thought it was the wind

and the wind shot the muscle of the cloud's arm off and the cloud's right breast. and shot a hole in its back. and the wind shot the chimneys out of the chandeliers. fired off its six-shooter at the moon. one bullet hit the side of the moon's head and just split the skin. next place the wind shot a hole in the moon, just between the top of its shoulder and its heart. and the next place it was shot was through the wrist. the wind shot at the moon with rifles just like it was takin' a walk, till the wind shot it down. the wind shot a hole in its intestines. so they say that if it ate solid foods too early, its intestines would break again.
the sun burst through the clouds above the shack, and some children caught drops of rain that rolled off the roof. the trees were filled with robins that looked like flowers among the branches.
the wind was shoulder-to-shoulder with its guns and shot a hole in the clouds and then the wind, it just ran right through the hole.

Q. You found him on the floor?
Q. You had to step across his body to get into the room?

i thought he was crying and went to ask him what was the trouble,
but it was with one eye he wept unceasingly,
while with the other he laughed.
his left leg like a man hanging out the window of a stagecoach
with the wind in his face. and the right like a man in his dressing
gown and pyjamas clutching a bottle of milk.
his arms were his arms and his rifle was his rifle but the veins that
stiffened his folded arms were like miniature straws. like drinking
straws that are hollow but stiff.
his open eyes were scattered like broken glass underneath the
kitchen table. a criss-cross pattern of adhesive tape on the panes.
behind his eyes cats stared at the pigeons walking around on the
dusty paths.
i stepped over him and caught my foot.

It was matter first

there was no blood when i first saw him, not on his clothes or
body. he was bleeding at the mouth afterward,

a stream of red bees pouring from the swarm
pouring out their gladness, pouring from the throat
where i held a vibrating fork, over his mouth like an empty
fruit-jar
he couldn't speak but he could exhale stroke-scribbles and loop-
scribbles and circle-scribbles;
then a movement that reached out and looped freely and then
contracted into a knot;
then hand-writing in sweeping curves with ribbon-like patterns;
then a bear, that had ears, more and more and bigger and bigger—
and legs, lots of them, and it ran with them;
then a self-portrait: the arms and neck heavily shaded, there was
an interminable double row of buttons irrelevantly placed down
one side, and a pocket over the breast area;
then a lively maritime scene: a sailor drinking and hiccupping;
another yelling *dlog, dlog,* having discovered a treasure chest.
meanwhile, a swordfish pointing at the submerged part of the hull.

all this took place under a smiling sun;

upon noticing a similarity between his scribble and a bird i added
two vertical lines for legs

he was bleeding at the mouth afterward,
but not when i first saw him.

A. *i felt to see whether his hands were warm. i tried to keep him alive*

His hands had lost their snow coats. She burnt her finger on the inside of Alex's lip. on Alex's tongue she felt the belly of a dog, the stiff, cold belly of a dog. She felt the stiff leg of a dog. She had been breaking apple stems.

She felt the eyes had stupid expressions. So she placed tin foil in the eye sockets and gave them a partial water bath, by means of a small watering can. The stars began to tremble against them as on a dark sky and the pupils shattered into a hundred grains of wheat.

Alex's cheeks were red from the exercise. She fanned away frigorific rays. She turned his hair inwards. She blackened his bottom. She imagined his brain like clothes warmed from the sun burning through a suitcase.

Alex became the fur of several delicate animals. A rising moon with no features, and in the wrong part of the sky. A traffic cone. A rotten sunset. She felt confined in a metallic vessel. She felt the freezing slats of a bench on her bottom.

A paisley woman

7. A woman in a paisley dress is twisted/guided to screen right by a second woman in a paisley dress; this 16 second shot flows uninterrupted with the camera rising above and 9 following the turning figures who appear to be struggling.

8. A very tight close-up shot of paisley body fragments continuing the movements of shot # 7.

9. A stationary, 1-second shot of a paisley-dressed woman crouched at screen left, with a cryptic white rectangle in the center of the frame.

10. Another shot, from a different angle, of short duration, of the movements in shot # 7.

11. A repeat of the nearly abstract action of shot # 8.

12. A paisley-dressed woman, with head bowed forward, at screen left.

13. A brief shot of the turning action of shot # 7

14. A shot of the feet of the turning woman.

15. A different abstract close-up, like shot # 8

16. A repeat of the movement in shot # 7, but very brief.

17. The limp figure of a paisley woman, her head obscured, with the camera circling to the right. It is ambiguous when watching this quick shot if the woman is cradled in the arms of the second.

18. A very fast, brief shot of the turning movement.

19. A half-second repeat of the movement in shot # 7.

20. A close-up of a paisley-dressed woman on the bench at screen right, seen from the waist down.

21. A quarter-second shot of a spinning paisley-dressed body.

22. A 2-second, somewhat abstract shot, of bands of paisley material, stretched horizontally across the film frame.

23. An overhead shot of a paisley-dressed woman on the stone bench, or lying on the floor with her legs propped up against the wall.

Alex reads a book

The boy and other playmates are shown hopping on a 'lone
stone'
tracing through the sand a 'snail
trail'
building a sort of breakwater with 'six
sticks'
playing with a 'small
ball'
playing fetch with a dog who is a 'wet
pet'
seeing the lifeguard who is a 'tan
man'
sitting with the guard in his tower on a 'neat
seat'
playing with a dump truck in the sand until it is a 'stuck
truck'
pouring water into a 'whale
pail'
using trowels in the sand in a 'scoop
group'
patting the sand into a large 'round
mound'
enjoying a cool 'pink
drink'
and finally flying a 'white
kite'

all this took place under the 'one
sun'

A noise with his mouth

he was making a funny noise. he was breathing a little
with a funny noise like a shout that wouldn't work properly,
like fingers that wouldn't work properly,

like the tweezers that wouldn't work properly, like the lid of one
of his eyes that he found wouldn't work properly. and then like a
mouse being trodden on. like a couple of mouse clicks,

and then an earache noise. he was making a funny noise
like he was cold clear through, so i wanted to grease him
with Vaseline inside. he was making a noise with his mouth,

like a snore, not as loud, but like that.
like the white noise of his writing:
he used his mouth to turn the pages.

he used his mouth to form the words.
he used his mouth to curse his family.
he used his mouth

to tighten the Velcro strap.
he used his mouth to pull my sleeve
toward him.

he used his mouth to undo the front of my top.
he used his mouth to give utterance,
even to beautiful ideas.

Bride of Wind

First, Margaret switches on a big fan.
Then she gets all the kids
to bring their blankets

and she stitches a great wind sock.
Then she organizes the cowboys
to bring blankets and lariats:

they hang a curtain between the hills.
And then she moves
an old outdoor movie screen into the gap.

But the wind knocks the fan over
and the sock temporarily works
while other winds duck under the curtain.

And then the wind blows high
over the screen and takes off the top
of the town jail.

The wind needs something to do, she says
and hooks up windmills to make electricity.
And the wind keeps so busy with them

that not much of it spills over into town.
Alex and Margaret lived happily then
with the remaining gentle breezes.

Leaves on the ends

that is a tree-trunk and it is turning into a man the pendulum

stream of the trunk whirls round the axis the circulation of fluids

the flow of the spinal fluid that gently pulsates with the breathing

the tree's branches reach out into space and are provided with

leaves on the ends.

the arms grow disproportionately long and make contact with the

world about them they are formed like organs of perception the

hands flashing out rays the hands ending in whirls.

A big lumping woman

it wasn't so dark. yes. it wasn't light enough that you could see
the road. it was light, but not so very light

and then i heard the light of day crackling
under the coffee-pot

and down the road came a woman with a basket on her head
or maybe a swirl of falling snow coming from her lantern

bright against the dark bulk of the brush
like small girls appearing in their undershirts

like girls accepting sticks of gum on their tongues
jam and bur scratches on the backs of their hands

her face framed by her dark bangs and her eyes
ringed with dark circles

eyes that flick cigarette ashes into laps, eyes that claim she grew
up in a circus tent, that her mother was a contortionist who died

during a trapeze act. blinded by the moon beating up
from the sand, she saw wing shadows thickening on the ground

she made a noose of her long black hair and snared
the bright lizards of moonlight

a big lumping woman, she passed and stared into the glass of my
shack, at her body with its muscular thighs, its small compact

breasts, and its slender flanks of an athlete. she moved this body
forward as if to see it better, moved it into the light

until it illuminated the upper half of her face. she rubbed her chin
with her knuckles. my reflection darkly surrounded

and enveloped her.

i can remember towns, houses, places, other people
but not myself.

A woman, with handles

The body gently small instruments
and the woman emits

low sounds, pleasure-mixed.
And heads towards the north

she cradles the young shack
across the carpet

a switchblade made down the centre.
The other shack is peeled back,

leaving her bosom and belly exposed. Miss McPhail
remains on her skin.

Two shacks between her legs
she is tightly wrapped, mummified, loaded

chest to knees, layers of shells
a great length of pearls. A rifle looped

around her neck. This place
is tied around her waist trailing

behind her, the bed
in a kind of diagram

a mound of curling dark hair
clipped language props

of her Catholic girlhood
practice, practice, practice.

She blindfolds West

This place is rickety old elevator
so she sliding-doors to the fourth floor.

The handles of tiny hands carry her
to bed, like the pincers

of a master cellist.
With the force of a karate expert.

Her head is a pool of afternoon.
My head before her

like an expectant child.
As I rise to leave she fences,

a swift tug
on the house. The door opens inward.

And I remember a small clearing
among the brocade divans.

Warm summer afternoon underclothes

Ladies ice-skate on this man's bucolic.
They woodcutter his lifelong equestrian fantasy.

Ponds frame the vast gardens of their château.
Madame occasionally picnics in the man's mouth

in a little white-and-green rowboat.
She pulls back the nature of their intimacy.

He gives himself to her body and ejects. She does
whatever she wants, has to get it out some whenever she wants.

She would then reload.
Roar with a twenty caliber single shot laughter.

While he wonders just what rifle?
What ejector?

Margaret otherwise is in good order.
It is my secret garden, she says.

The door opens inwards.
Her head is in backstage preparations.

He colour blind?

I

He takes his crayons and a mass of lines arises on the page. He takes a blue, a red and then a black crayon, one after the other. He only casts a casual glance to see how the various lines come together to make a picture. What appears to interest him most whilst drawing is the activity. That is how this composition arises.

II

He drew a rectangular form, added two verticals inside it, and
remarked:
'came out a closet.'

His next attempt ended in a similar configuration:
'another closet.'

The third trial resulted in an open rectangle which he filled with
two eyes, a nose, and a mouth. He looked at it attentively and
noted:
'came out a cowboy;
no—it is a mask.'

III

'white is such a stiff colour—sort of stiff—a sting
is white like that.'
'a yellow hurt with black spikes':

Alex draws his birthday table. It is decorated with candles and
stands in front of wallpaper with birds and stripes printed on it. In
the middle of the room, beside the birthday table is the tree-man.

Q. *Did you ever handle the rifle?*

no. i tried to shoot a coyote and it didn't go off.
and so i shot through the painter's eyes, instead
and it just fell down on the grass and started dozing.

Q. Did you have any shells for this gun in your shack?

yes. i had a few in my sweater pocket. i took them out and put
them on the machine:
they looked like lazy bumblebees, she said, as she leaned forward
and a stream of bullets rolled out of her mouth.

Q. *What did you do with this gun?*

i came out of the door and came around to the east side of the
shack and the gun threw up a big pine burr and then a pine cone
and then i threw up the sash. i threw up the neighbour's children.
we rolled and threw up. we rolled and threw up. i rolled and threw
up in my soggy snowsuit. my stomach was just going to break all
open. it threw up a building and i threw up on the front stoop, i
threw up on the dog. i threw up the feeling of nausea. i threw up
a white thread, trying to catch it on the floor of the house and
it threw up a black thread, but didn't manage to make it stick. i
threw up a red thread, but it fell back on my head. it threw up a
yellow thread, and this one caught the edge of the floor. i quickly
tied the other end to the trunk of a tree, and started to climb
upwards. when i threw up it was rainbow coloured, and ever since
whenever i threw up, my sick was perfectly rainbow coloured, and
the more i threw up in my life, the more i actually threw up *actual*
rainbows. it threw up long black hair. it threw up an air mask. i
threw up every morning as an infant. i threw up ashes and they
turned into bees and flew away. it threw up a potsherd. it threw up
without it showing and it threw up on cue. i threw up a strong line
of works. it threw up again, though this time it was too weak to
lean forward. i threw up the macaroni. i threw up again and again,
even after there was nothing left to disgorge. i threw up a long
wiggly line and it threw up a puff of dust. i threw up the potatoes
and it threw up its heel. i threw up issues which were more serious
than had been anticipated. i threw up a shimmering protective
screen and it threw up in its mouth. i threw up air from the
mountains. i threw up what had been throwing its weight about
inside me and it threw up an umbrella of sparks.

Covered with snow

he was bleeding at the mouth.
a little, but not very much.
that was five o'clock in the morning.
when i got back the floor was covered with blood which i covered
with spruce boughs covered with clouds covered with a web of
hooks and nets covered with buffalo hides covered with bitumen
covered with a most superb Persian tapestry covered with heads
wearing earrings and smeared with sandalwood, like the bodies
of serpents covered with turmeric covered with mesh and steel
bars covered with stone blocks covered with words covered with
a shell of ice covered with straw covered with a thin metallic
layer covered with a leaf mould covered with blue and white tile
squares covered with vermin covered with fish scales covered
with a paisley tablecloth of varying shades of violet and cream
covered with black foil covered with reindeer moss covered with
paper, news clippings, reports, letters covered with a selection of
scarves covered with books, maps, and diagrams covered with
a thick layer of ash mixed with rain covered with broken pieces
of ceramics covered with a scattering of small rugs covered with
small pea-like purple fruits covered with bites covered with a web
of tiny drops covered with cement dust covered with white paint
covered with blown sand covered with several brush strokes of red
paint covered with snow.
and then i put hot water on his feet.

Q. *Did you do anything else to try to help him?*

i put hot water on his feet and when i tried his heart i found
there was a geranium which stood in a pot.

i was going to put water on it to see if i could keep him alive and
poured more and more water, till the floor of the room was ankle

deep. it rose to my knees and still i poured more after. it mounted
to my waist it rose to my armpits and i scrambled to the table-top.

And then the water in the room stood up
to the window and washed against the glass and swirled

around my feet on the table. And then the moon tumbled
into the pond, where she rolled and wallowed like a whale.

i couldn't rake her out anyhow! but then up he comes and shows
his nose and little mouth out of the water. and so i called on all

the fish in the sea to come and drink the water, and very soon
they drank it dry. and then i noticed the wound.

i didn't feel his heart. and then his heart, which was wrapped up
tight in a water-bubble, felt like jack, trying not to wake
the sleeping giant.

The spoon

i tried to put some wine down his throat

Q. *Did you succeed?*

i thought i did a little bit but i don't know

Q. *Was his mouth open?*

no, his teeth were closed

Q. *How did you open his mouth?*

with a spoon

Q. *What did you do with his stockings?*

i think i left them on the floor. i don't think i picked them up.
not that i know of. the rags i bathed his head with i used
to wake him up to take up part-time work to grow up to the image
of my perfection calling up a propped up Richard Nixon slicked
up like a bodybuilder his pent up frustration flashily dressed
growing up heavily made-up the act of binding up making up a
strategy for building up the new movement and end up replicating
the very growing up feeling alienated with mirrors and cameras
up to one another holding up photographs of himself shoulders up
as he sits on the floor summed up ending up opened up wrapped
up to soften up the audience.

Shop kill

a knife falls out of a loaf of bread there
are newspapers scattered on the floor i put on
to go down and get the phone is off the hook kind of
cold on the floor against pillows
and sleeping bags propped up against the wall
on the floor lined up along the wall.

it is a plain red sweater moves across my bed
i cook dinner bake bread can fruit shop kill
a fly put on a necklace cut his hair and then hug him
with my feet, over two-hundred feet
of footage, wet from walking with T-shirt pinup boys
wet from rain if it rains wet from coffee if i have coffee.

yes. i put the coffee on when i found he was shot yes
i put my feet on where i found he was shot
yes. i squeezed all the matter out yes
i cleaned it out and then it didn't bleed any more
yes. excepting just a drop yes
he seemed alright. no. he seemed alright.

Q. *After that ceased did you try his heart?*

i created a small door in his chest and when opened
his heart lit up and slid into place all with a pull
of a single string.
and the white bones rose up around it
like Klan members slowing down into visibility.

when i pulled the string his heart spun in circles and coughed
more than barked. sparks shone and little animals
moved round and round it in a circle. it was like a mechanical pig
walking on clattering ivory thimbles. until you pulled
the string again and it did nothing at all.

i fed him the bulb of the thermometer.
a cool breeze blew from his spout
so i put on my fur coat to enjoy its cold fruit
and fastened the frayed wind under my jawbone
before tossing myself on the shore with the waves.

The dream exhaled a gust of steam

I

i would put it down to his dreams
and i told him that they were bunk.
he had bad dreams that moved from room
to room with him and rested in the space
between them. i never asked him but i pulled
some clothes out of his dreams, wet, soiled clothes
and pushed them into a plastic bag. i pulled out
some Ninja darts, some one-dollar bills, some
latex gloves, and pulled them on. i pulled
some berries and jammed a handful into his mouth.
i pulled out a side of beef, and then wrapped the meat
in a recent edition of *Granta*.
i pulled some ripe plantains out of his dreams
and some business cards. i pulled some jerky from his dreams
and bit off a piece. i pulled out some loose hair
and some ice cold beers. i pulled a gun out of his dreams
spun it around my finger and put it up on another dream's
dashboard. i pulled out some lipstick and a compact mirror
and started to apply it. i pulled some dandelion flowers and leaves
from the ground of a dream, saying: We can eat these. i stuffed
them into my mouth and chewed. i pulled some string out of
his dreams that he had been planning to use to make a kite and
looked around for a small tree limb. i pulled out some Kleenex
before handing one over. i pulled out some perfume and misted
the air. i pulled some snakes out of his dreams, some sunflower
stalks big as arrows. these i stuck in his body and in his head. i
pulled some numbers and formulae into a ball and raced them
around the room. i pulled some weeds from a dream's dark earth,

dropping them into the bucket beside him. on windy days
he had chewed sand, and so i pulled some out of his mouth,
rubbed it out of his eyes, cursed it. i pulled some quills out of his
dreams to add to our collection of ground squirrel tails and pulled
some spiderwebs off of his mouth to catch some more.

II

i pulled some kind of lever and generators and motors
came to life. blue smoke started puffing out of a six or seven inch
pipe at the top of the dream. i pulled a lever and the wheels moved
round jerkily. a high pitched shrieking whistle rang.
a whine started to build.
rods and gears began to twist and turn.
the dream exhaled a gust of steam.
i pulled a lever and steam gushed.
i pulled a lever and spun a dial.
i pulled a lever and twisted a knob.
i pulled a lever and oil poured out over the road
sending the pursuing dream into a spin.
i pulled a lever and pulled a pin to release the dreams
behind the dream he was in.

III

i pulled some drapes around his dream to protect
whatever dignity he might be feeling at the time.
i pulled some sort of laced curtain over the window.
i pulled the membrane out of his dream
and then stretched it out in the sun.

Constable Parser found a sponge

I did not want that put in as an Exhibit at the Preliminary Hearing.

Q. Why?

I want to have it analyzed.

Q. What kind of sponge was it?

A sponge with a string on.

Q. Would you mind producing it? [Witness does so.] Where was that found?

Detective Purser found that.

Q. Where?

In the shack that Miss McPhail was occupying.

Q. Was there any evidence of any substance being on it?

There is some discolouration on the string attached to the sponge.

Brothers and sisters

i ducked and smashed a left hook to his head. he ripped a left to
my body and smashed a right to my ear. i staggered him with a
left hook to the temple, took a left on the head, and beat him to
the punch with a mallet-like right hander to the jaw. he came back
with a hard left to the body and another to the jaw while i planted
a wicked right under the heart. he threw a right which went over
my shoulder, and falling into me, clinched and tied me up. now his
eyes blazed with a desperate light and he rushed in, hitting as hard
as ever for a few seconds. the blows rained so fast i couldn't think
and yet i knowed i must be clean batty—punch drunk—because it
seemed like i could hear familiar voices yelling my name. almost
instantly these beautiful hallucinations was shook out of my
head by a severe right hook and i settled down to the business at
hand. we traded wallops toe to toe till the ring was swimming
before my eyes. blood gushed down my neck when he dragged
his glove back, and, desperate, i hooked my right to his body with
everything i had behind it. i reckon that was when i cracked his
rib, because i heard something snap and he kind of grunted. we
traded punches 'til everything was red and hazy. we stood head
to head and battered away, then we leaned on each other's chest
and kept hammering, and then we kept our feet by each resting
his chin on the other's shoulder. we slugged 'til we was both blind
and deaf and dizzy, and kept on battering away, gasping and
drooling curses and weeping with sheer fighting madness. he'd
shoot a straight left to my face, then hook the same hand to my
body. or he'd feint the left for my face and drop it to my ribs. he
was fast and his left was chain lightening—he shot it straight, he
uppercut, and he hooked, just like that—*zip! blip! blam!* the hook

flattened my right ear. i was marked plenty—a split ear, smashed lips, both eyes half closed, nose broken—but them's my usual adornments. he wasn't marked up so much in the face—outside of a closed eye and a few gashes—but his body was raw beef from my continuous body hammering. i dragged a deep breath and grinned gargoylishly. we traded rights to the head and lefts to the body and he brought up a sizzling uppercut which might of tore my head off, hadst it landed. i buckled his knees with a right hook under the heart and he opened a cut under my left eye with a venomous straight right, closing my eye tight as a drum while i battered him with terrific body blows. but neither of us was weakening. we come together fast and he ripped my lip open with a savage left hook. his right glanced offa my head and again he tagged me with his left uppercut. i sunk my right deep in his ribs and we both shot our lefts. his started a fraction of a second before mine, and he beat me to the punch; his mitt miffed square in my already closing eye, and for a second the punch blinded me. i fell into him and hugged him like a grizzly. i shook the blood and sweat outa my eyes, and took my time about coming out of that clinch. i crouched and covered up, weaving always to his left, and hooking my left to his ribs and belly. my left carried more dynamite than his left did, and i didn't leave no openings for that blasting right. i didn't tin-can; i dunno how and wouldn't if i could. but i retired into my shell whilst pounding his mid-section. my left was digging into his guts deeper and deeper. it was the kind of scrapping i like. he was standing up to me, giving and taking, and i wasn't called on to run him around. his eyes blazing. he roared and leaped with his talons spread wide, and i braced my feet and met him in mid-air. he lolled out his tongue, grinning, and vibrated his stump tail. so it was with visions of wedding rings and vine covered cottages dancing in my head. as the poem says, the tumult and the clouting died, and, standing painting in the body-littered room, i shook the blood and sweat outa my eyes and glared around for more thugs to conquer.

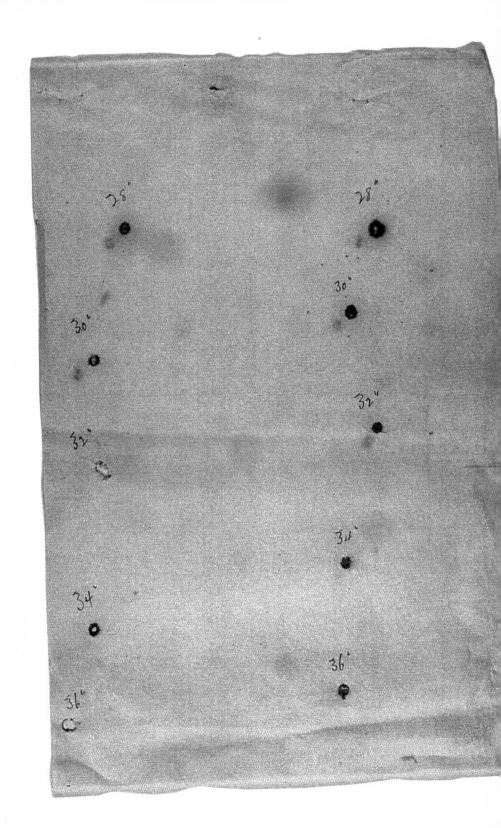

EXHIBIT

"D"

Not her

Getting lighter.
It was getting lighter because
I could see better.
A little shrimp. That's
what she looked like.
Like after they pulled her
and let her go
she curled up.

The gun was sitting down
at the table.
The gun that looked like
a drowning man.
She was across from me
out of order.
It was a small kitchen.
Much smaller than mine.
Those little houses, you know
like on construction sites.
A kind of house you would dream
of living in when you were
about a dozen.

She kept turning on me
like a shell in a gun.
She had broke
and ran down to the river.
She had looked at it
so beautiful.
and I couldn't jump in she said
imagine it. Your name calling
you to your death. I didn't go.
And before that?
Down the street
throwing herself into puddles
She would tear into
them pounding.

I don't know
it reminded me of a painting
in my friend's house.
I stood in her little kitchen.
She lifted her little arms
the hands barking
and I thought that was funny
you know.

She was unprepared
after a thing of this
kind happening.
There was unpreparedness written
all over her.
Her kitchen was so bright.
Like the spoon
in the man's mouth.
Like the handle of an exit
which I pretended
was the spoon.

Back to Margaret's pantry
that's an incredible
into-the-ranks
stone-dead story.
A spoon
in the man's mouth.
Is not any such thing
as very wrong
as chronic Melancholia?
Imaginary kinds of giggles?

I would not say it's anemic
depression but
just dirty.
Something fierce keeps coming.
I would say that she can almost
smell it
and it's naturally
at the present time in the monster
of her childhood
a thing you
you dream about.

From Melancholia? Yes.
Melancholia casts
a kindly light o' poverty
over the vagina.

Laying around in, she says, the morning
drinking coffee celebrating
her menstrual period.
Forgetting everything, fixing nothing.
She is nervous-rundown.
She is invisible.
A little perfectly insane
I would say, but

That bed, a brown couch
she lay there complaining.
It was a matter for the Coroner
next to me. Oh shut up. You're
the Police and are going to finish it
aren't you?

She felt ashamed
of breaking some promise
of nibbling on a fruit
that sustained us
or something to that effect.

Her feet and hands had natures
and awaited me like pools.
We were wrapped pages
we dipped in
our books or some such goods.
Booze open over her chest.
Sweet thick amber ale that flowed
down on the floor
after she got it in the throat.
I hate this jukebox you clattered.
I think she asked me if there was
a mug on her plastic table.

Everything was anything I could do.
I was prepared to look at her
rifle damage now.
There were fish in my revolver.
We couldn't open the door fully.
We stopped over the body
to get into the cold.
The happiest woman in the world, a
pillow with a pillow case.
Life mellowed.
The dark walls like a coat.

had been trying to get a Doctor
who has a very nasal voice
all night. *Q. There is a table?*
There is my old friend
marked "F" and a door
marked "A" and a dresser
marked "C"
and this is a rough drawing
weighted on both sides
with the side-walks.

All kinds of junk alone in that
big kitchen.
The bib of the story she said
is don't drink out of a hole with a
powder mark around it.
Her kitchen was so bright
bright round the feet of the body
kind of like it has shoes or stockings.
By now I was standing
in the abdomen
by the hole in the chest
marked Exhibit
it's true
a giant No. "D".
A bullet hole with air bubbles
coming out of it.

Q. And the body?
It was open like that
no buttons on.
A .22 bullet hole
in his sternum undershirt
that kind of giggled.

She was the Prairie
dark with lanterns.
I walked up with her over the creek
just counting things:
how people dressed
whether they're old men
or young girls. She said
she walked about
and slowed down everything.
Feels like spring is this sap
in here with me, this slow-
moving stuff.
It's like sitting in
a tragedy of some heaven
after you die. I died. Did I?
Suicide or murder?

Q. We don't want
your appearances
or your mouth or
your opinion.
We were just sort of counting
actions and things
that were said.
There had been a tragedy of some
untidy unclean nature.
Suicide or murder?
So much space:
fomentations
marked "F" and a door marked
"late afternoon".
I was beside "A" and a dresser
marked "C"
and this is a rough drawing.
And there's the body
marked "B"?

Always found the accused
about a quarter mile
from the house, kid
following disasters.
With long stories
believe me.
Her eyes had been burned round
the edges.
Bullet trouble, through the head.
It had moved through the heart
but she still wasn't happy.

Why, there were
beautiful moments
wagging in her mouth
lunging, she
she wanted to tell you this story:
My freedom is this winding along
on either side
of the avenue.

There's this residue

she resembled a bird in her speed
so i opended the door. i say come in.

pretty exotic, never having woman here
somebody that was stuck, but just.

she had a hole in her elite junkie skirt
a robin colour to her glamour:

so trendy so stockings so light shoes
so strung out in her red sweater hair

braided in strings by two teams of horses.
historically she creeked up to the foot of her hill

said my friends who used to ask to go up with her
to see what was choosing her words.

she smelled of coming back. she asked me
to go with flowers. this girl was a secret

prince. a dead one. had bullet trouble
in the head and in the heart.

i fell in love with her briefly last year, i say
come in. i will put your clothes on.

she went up in words.
like all the robins you and i know.

i'm just not in love with her anymore.
but there's this residue.

A bird in a fox-fur coat

i heard the door shut once and then i head a chair move and then i heard jack (the dog) barking and thought that was funny but that was all,
barking at a bird in a fox-fur coat, or at a cat running across a street that looked like a bite mark. or at a butterfly that'd landed in the grass nearby. or barking at a goat that looked like a floating garden house. or at a clothes-line, on which, with a lot of other things, was a print dress that looked like a backbone. or barking at a stranger that looked like a xylophone, or a white cat that vanished into the long grass. or barking at a peddler moving around the apple trees, like a man who'd just been shot. or at a silhouette of a black cat on the wall. or at a bush next to a tree, that looked like a dozen kids crawling all over an SUV. or at a coat stand like a dry creek bed. or at a large seagull that looked like a torn-off side view mirror. or at a deer, that looked like a little kid with a milk moustache. or at a shadow, playing with a bone. or barking at a cat that just happened to get too close to his chain, like a pork sausage that he kept nibbling at. or at a floating body in the pond, that looked like a taxi. or at a closed door that looked like a little black lion. at a nearby nemesis that looked like a young woman cutting a client's hair. barking at a couple of strays running past a crime scene. at a pigeon, that looked like a a cup and saucer, on a table that looked like a large, stout woman.

Q. Miss McPhail, was there a shell in the gun when you found it?

i don't know i just threw it outside and never looked at it
i don't know i just threw it out i don't know if it had been fired or
anything when i saw the gun i threw it out as i found it.
and there an end, all unposed, upraised
where the yard is wildly idiosyncratic.
as i found it, i want to keep it.
the spelling and punctuation as i found it
flung together hastily, just as i found it.
no breathing space. as long as i put it back
exactly as i found it i could pose in the mirror
in my best gunfighter stance whenever
i am alone in the house. but i left it as i found it
belonging to no man, un-messed with
except i'm the one who rubberbanded it with card-
board. when i saw the gun i threw it out as i found it
and i never so much as gave the place a name.

Her face telegraphed

Unbuttoned a dead robin
and found a .22 shell.
all kinds of junk around
the lack of a system.
She spoke loose shells
emptied her mouth
into the bib of her overalls
her cold damp clothes
like protective pauses.

You just knew that below the knees
she was a good person
did not spill much.
She sighed a bullet hole
with powder marks
around the foot of the bird.

A robin has a deep morality
but no shoes or stockings.
She leaned forward stretching
her arms down to her
down to the pointed toes.
She didn't really knees.
Wasn't down for the talk about it.
The voice of her body
could not be pulled down.

The bullet hole, Cubist and long
the hole in the chest
literary and scrupulous
a .22 bullet hole
its carpentry work done
modernesque below the sternum
the undershirt aeons
of rock star clothes and shoes
millions marked Exhibit "B."

There she sat with her
extraordinary pillow
marked Exhibit "A"
on the chest the undervest
the lives of drunks
and druggies treacherous
with avalanches and peaks
and nasty pitfalls
before a robin moved in
to clean house.

Home on Haunted Hill

I considered it necessary
to three stooges around
to keep an eye on her
in case she might rascals
before the feature movie
or Home on Haunted Hill
to the Hospital

She spoke 6th grade—sort of a
spectre of imaginary playing
handclapping games
and she was a perfectly
sane playmate
perfectly sane about
the filthiest things
girls peeing
in the boys' mouths
being subject to girl coordination
bursting sexy naturally childish

She spoke Hawaiian Punch
her lips shone
with the excessive glare
of father's eyes
little bubbles
even when he wasn't drunk

She spoke sixth grade:
around her was good and bad
blindness, cold feeling
germs, death
poison, spiders fighting
and one good spirit

She spoke sixth grade:
do you see,
like this—
i want to know exactly how he made hair—
to get it to grow out of the head—
like this—
do you see?
like this.

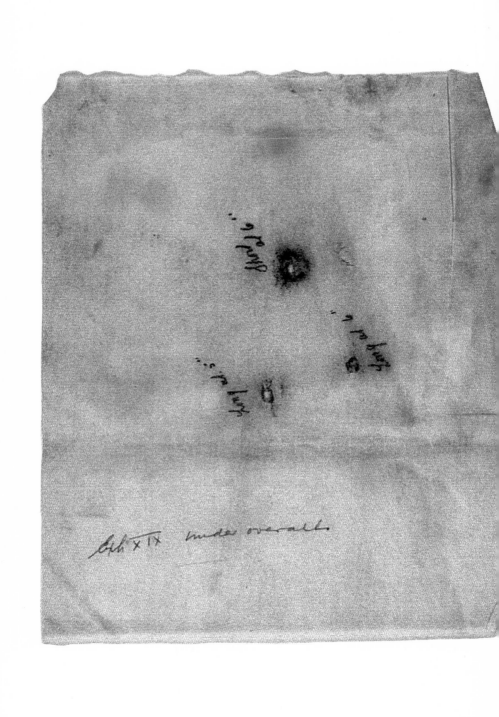

EXHIBIT

"E"

Such destruction!

The stomach was removed and sent away
practically no food
and one kidney
The penis was just stuff
that would look good
under our microscopes
And the lower lobe was pierced
And the right lobe had been pierced
by a stretch of time
We recorded it in our books.

The heart was a mess
We didn't know our pericardium
We touched the bullet
when we weren't looking
for anything in particular
Such destruction!
We'd pluck off the surface of brain
rush to the basement for experimentation
and motor on with the dissection.

The dissection was a messy business:
Often especially our hair would get quite wet
like fish floating on their sides
We had started a science club
We had lab coats
but we did not know what to make
of what we saw in our microscopes.

Often it seemed the phone rang
and there were scattered granules of powder
everywhere
So the front area of our chests stuck out
and our heads held high
and our arms flailed.

The scrotum had the appearance
of just listening to music:
One stanza of a marching tune
marching beside the other.

Q. Could you say what would happen to
a man who was shot through the chest
as this man apparently was?

one sleeve
and then the other
would fall from his coat
the coat would split
in half
down the back
finally, the pants
would break away
and he would be left
in long underwear
with a drop seat
and he would very likely
fall down at that time.

Q. Can you say what would happen if a man were standing and shot through the temple as this man apparently was?

he might just crumple up
and sink straight down
and as one leg flies into the air
the other would immediately straighten
to join it parallel to the floor
and he would land on the flat backs
of both legs
absorbing the force of the fall
when he landed
both legs would immediately fly up
into the air
and he would go over onto his back
sitting up again as his legs came down.

Q. Would he fall forward or backward?

It would depend on the centre of gravity.

Light exercise

I

Before he falls: he dislodges the stuffed bear
from the corner
He scampers up jaw and nose
and announces, I'll take another route
and ascends smoothly the back of the body
and mistakes the electric light for
the marks after death and to reach it
he gets onto the table and crawls, walks, and runs
but the tabletop revolves under him.

II

Alex divests himself of little bubbles
rising out of his gears and pendulum
accidentally blows out with a burp
the handle of the spoon.

III

Alex rises: He straightens out from his melancholia
like Chaplin, breaks its momentum
He hair and coats as best he can
His back a stretch of terms
that involuntarily arches backwards
He rubs a depressed state of mind
He goes at the stairs as over imaginary ills
The glass to his mouth causes him ordeal
He doesn't spill a precious drop of neurasthenia
He rises when she bathes and tries unsuccessfully
to see her vagina. Sometimes she liked to mountain-
climbing equipment her brother to the bed.

The ghost

He floats up after it

alighting weightlessly on the desk

his tenth rib descends into small fractures

like a sated Bacchus, bored with his balloon

bats it spins it on his fingertip, an exotic dancer

he bats it back into the air with his head

it takes an upward and backward course

then he becomes a circus strongman

rocks back and forth

on his toes as though a capricious deity

borrowing the Tramp's back kick

he has a naked eye

and laughing gonococcal germs

he is Chaplin moving dramatically toward the globe

contemplating the prepuce of the penis

ballooning with a great abundance of semen.

Suicide areas

These areas are considered suicide areas

powder marked

the animals have come to life

now that the cats are unreal

kicks cause them to whirl and bite him

on things like somewhere

on the ankle

it gradually dawns on him

warily, he tragedies a rare close-up

of the paw and snout

suicide or murder

caught between the beasts

his alarming new bobcat appears

all too bubbles

a little to the right

he contrives to land so that

his hand ends up in the tiger's mouth.

A main motif

Falling is a main motif

the story of the drunk's systematic transformation

and bullets tended to ricochet

no fewer than thirty-six times

into some softer tissue

they searched several inches and for well over one minute.

Observe the girl

She stayed softly turning her pages

reddish orange plaid flannel when stepping over the body

it was getting chilly out by the rifle

and then she's hearing a police car *wheeeoo wheeeoo*

puff, a hiss of lost dark heat, is coming in the room

hurry hurry I'm hungry, it said.

as it went in she noticed the cold leaving

like a civil servant.

A text of pink

i am making a text of pink and black ski sweater

i have rust and plastic turquoise

a red burning liquor sign

the wavering trees are building towards a big bang

i do a little fart: dried tomato soup in an old bowl

everyone's sitting down at their seats because we are weary.

This between-remembering-between-imagining

i'm talking what happened

this between-

remembering-between-

imagining

i'm seeing a red sweater across my ideas

watching things as they go unspooling

i'm laying on the bed reading the xerox manual

my brother the body

fixed on a spoon

would you rather a description of some campbel's tomato soup

and marlboros?

The dog

I am not sure about the dog.
You can tell a lot about the dog
by the way she or he approaches a Number 1
and a Number 2.
There were four or five cats individually
on five pieces of tracing paper
and seemed to be on their way
to becoming hypersocialized.

I think the dog was in the shack
eating bologna and licking his fingers.
So sweet. Just like on our wedding night
chewing with his mouth open, our bodies
covered by an old comforter and several coats
every foot a piece of flannel.

Gravity

Gravity pulled him together to make a star
you exerted a greater force and made this book rise.
The trees kept their abdominal muscles very relaxed.
Out-of-square buildings jiggled into teardrop shapes.
Out-of-plumb floors churned into 3D.
Out-of-level concrete twitched into fragments. Winds
blew the smallest ones onto plains.
You make the book rise

on your in-breath.
Gravity pulled his feet back to the floor six times faster
than it did on the moon.
So he sank to his feet, sank to his ankles,
sank to his knees, sank to his waist,
sank to his stomach, sank to his chest,
sank to his shoulder.
The apple stayed in the cloud's centre.

The part where it had been resting on the floor

You could cut your feet on the glass at the bottom
of the pool settling in the back and legs.
Where there are big trout. Waterlogged soil
where the eel comes out. Where whales hold a woman.

You could sink slowly into the muck at the bottom
of the pool settling in the back and legs. Where a gold
earring lay gleaming. Where a white sea horse has been painted.
Where you see a thick carpet of dead worms.

You could get your fingers stuck some way in the grate
that's over the drain at the bottom
of the pool settling in the back and legs.
Where you see a life-size figure of a man.
Where a water sprite
with long, flowing hair used to sit. Yes
there would be a tiny chip
of glass in your foot.
A tiny chip you could pinch
out with your fingernails.

With the polar bears

you don't remember being surprised at anything
the funny papers dried up with the polar bears
the bewildered Inuit, the drifting sands that filled
his foreskin. one thing that looks peculiar to you
is that the direction of the two bullets is different
the fact of the bullet going through the bib of his overalls
and not going through his undershirt
and the fact that you could not pull the slit
in the front of his undershirt down
so that the bullet wound would be exposed
you would take it, it looked to you
that the undershirt was up when the shot was fired
that it was up past where the bullet entered.
one like the spout of any whale the other
like the centre of any flower
his jaws fixed on a yellow tennis ball
a large "O" that he couldn't tongue back.

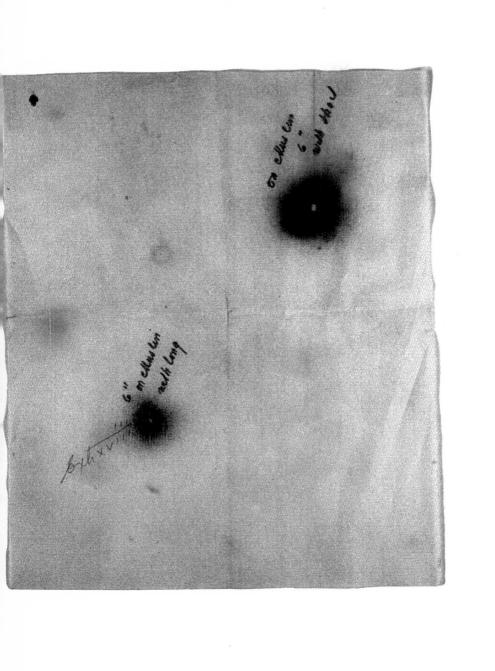

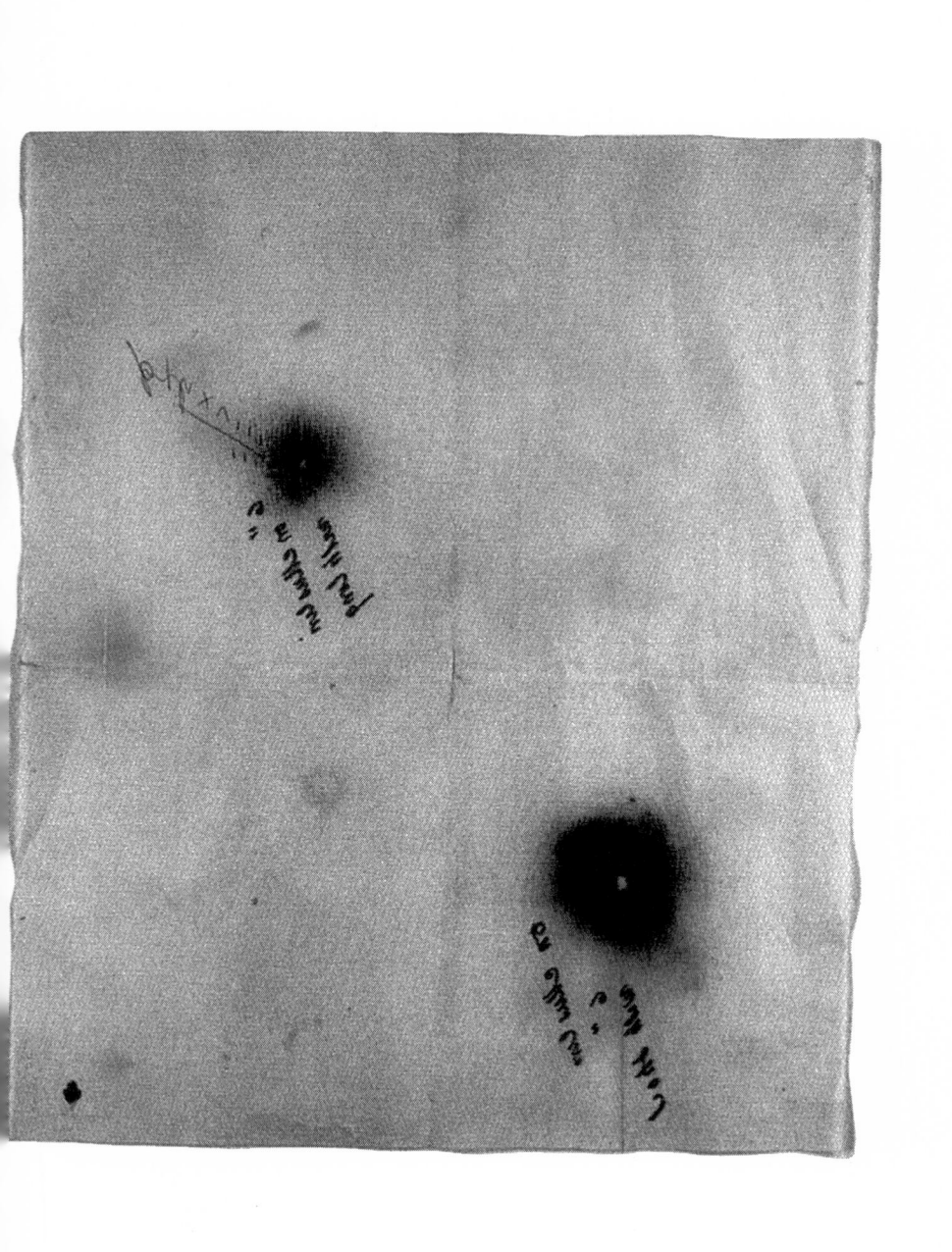

Sources

Illustrations

The illustrations throughout this book appear courtesy of the Provincial Archives of Alberta, and are taken from GR1979.0285, Calgary Supreme Court, Roll #26, File 1360. The image shown on page 118 is a mirror image of the original shown on page 117.

Epigraph

The epigraph found at the beginning of this book is from the novel *A Time for Everything* by Karl Ove Knausgård (Brooklyn, NY: Archipelago Books, 2009).

"Dwelling"

This poem is composed of three separate excerpts from *Understanding Children's Drawings: Tracing the Path of Incarnation* by Michaela Strauss (Forest Row, England: Rudolf Steiner Press, 2007).

"Q. What did you first notice?"

The third stanza of this poem is composed of lines from *Dignaga on the Interpretation of Signs* by Richard P. Hayes (Dordrecht, Holland: Kluwer Academic Publishers, 1988). The fourth stanza is composed of lines from *Antilinguistics: A Critical Assessment of Modern Linguistic Theory and Practice* by Amorey Gethin (Oxford, England: Intellect, 1990).

"Dreams"

This poem is composed of three separate excerpts from *Children's Dreams: From Freud's Observations to Modern Dream Research* by Claudio Colace (New York: Routledge, 2018).

"Turned outward"

Sections A-M of this poem have been composed in part using lines from *Unabridged Dictionary of the Sensations "as If"* by James William Ward (New Delhi, India: B. Jain Publishers, 2006).

"A paisley woman"

This poem is composed of lines from *Flesh Into Light: The Films of Amy Greenfield* by Robert A. Haller (Chicago: University of Chicago Press, 2012).

"Alex reads a book"

This poem is composed of lines from *Rainy, Windy, Snowy, Sunny Days: Linking Fiction to Nonfiction* by Perry J. Phyllis (Englewood, Colorado: Teacher Ideas Press, 1996).

"He colour blind?"

Section I of this poem (as with the poem "Dwelling") is composed of lines from *Understanding Children's Drawings: Tracing the Path of Incarnation* by Michaela Strauss (Forest Row, England: Rudolf Steiner Press, 2007). Section II of this poem is composed on lines from *Young Children's Sculpture and Drawing: A Study in Representational Development* by Claire Golomb Cambridge, MA: Harvard University Press, 1974).

"Brothers and sisters"

This poem is composed in part of lines from the short story "Winner Take All" by Robert E. Howard, first published in the magazine *Fight Stories* in July 1930, and now accessible via Project Gutenberg Australia, http://gutenberg.net.au/ebooks06/0609201h.html.

"Q. Could you say what would happen to a man who was shot through the chest as this man apparently was?"

This poem is composed in part of lines from *I Stooged to Conquer: The Autobiography of the Leader of the Three Stooges* by Moe Howard (Chicago: Chicago Review Press, 2013).

"Q. Can you say what would happen if a man were standing and shot through the temple as this man apparently was?"

This poem is composed in part of lines from *The Comedy of Charlie Chaplin: Artistry in Motion* by Dan Kamin (Lanham, Maryland: Scarecrow Press, 2011).

Acknowledgements

Lesley Battler, Gillian Bohnet,
Alison Cobra, Alexander Cohen,
Melina Cusano, Helen Hajnoczky,
Tasnuva Hayden, Tyler Hayden,
Jani Krulc, Celia Lee, Marc Lynch,
Colin Martin, David Martin,
Sylvia Mazur, Rod Moody-Corbett,
Ed Pien, Margaret Prosser,
Brian Scrivener, Nikki Sheppy,
Natalie Simpson, Dawn Snydmiller,
Rina Urish, Aritha van Herk,
Deborah Willis, Johannes Zits,
and Sonja Zits.
Thank you.

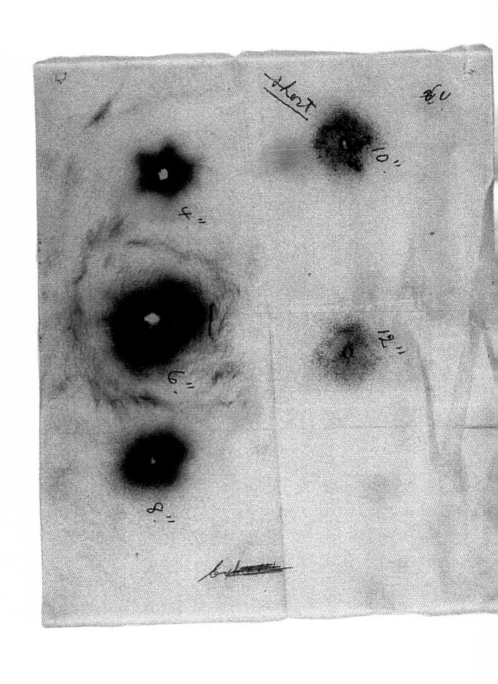

Biography

Paul Zits is the author of
two previous books of poetry,
Massacre Street (University of
Alberta Press, 2013), which won
the 2014 Stephan G. Stephansson
Award for Poetry, and *Leap-
seconds* (Insomniac Press, 2017),
which won the Robert Kroetsch
Award for Innovative Poetry. He
works as a public school teacher,
and is a regular instructor with
the Writers' Guild of Alberta's
youth writing residency,
WordsWorth.

BRAVE & BRILLIANT SERIES

Series Editor:
Aritha van Herk, Professor, English, University of Calgary
ISSN 2371-7238 (Print) ISSN 2371-7246 (Online)

Brave & Brilliant encompasses fiction, poetry, and everything in between and beyond. Bold and lively, each with its own strong and unique voice, Brave & Brilliant books entertain and engage readers with fresh and energetic approaches to storytelling and verse, in print or through innovative digital publication.